Masterpieces

Gramn

LOWER JUN

Diana Bentley and Dee Reid

Contents

Name ______________________ Date ____________

Diagnostic assessment – Nouns

Underline the **nouns**.

cat	house	door	jump	tree	good
far	table	dog	pen	look	what

Set A pages 3 - 4

Underline the **proper nouns**.

London	door	December	teacher	Mrs Moon
Dr Patel	Wednesday	computer	book	Sam

Set B pages 5 - 6

Underline all the **nouns** in the following sentences.

Mrs Smith went to the shop to get some eggs.

The children went to play on the swings in Green Park.

The headteacher gave Pradeep and Ann a badge for working hard.

Bouncy, the dog, ran off down the fields and over the river.

Set C pages 7 - 8

Name ______________________ Date ____________

Nouns

A **noun** is the **name of anything**. *Man, hat* and *book* are all **nouns**.

1 Look at the picture.
Find 10 **nouns** and write them in the spaces below.

_________ _________ _________ _________ _________

_________ _________ _________ _________ _________

2 Now put a **noun** in each sentence.

The _________ is on the wall.

The boy has a _________ and a _________.

A bird is in the _________ and the _________ is shining.

The _________ has a dog on a lead.

The _________ can see the cat on the _________.

Name ______________________________ Date ______________

Nouns

A **noun** is the **name of anything**. *Man, hat* and *book* are all **nouns**.

1 Underline ten different **nouns** in the story.

At the seaside

We went to the beach. I took my bucket and spade. I made a sand-castle and I put a flag on it and shells around it. My mum gave us a picnic. I asked Mum what was in the sandwiches. "They have egg in them," said Mum. "And sand as well," I said.

2 Write the correct **noun** next to each picture.

Name ______________________ Date ____________

Proper nouns

People's names, places, days of the week and months of the year are **proper nouns**. All **proper nouns** start with a **capital letter**.

1 Write in the answers.

The day after Thursday ____________

The month before April ____________

The name of your teacher ____________

The name of a river ____________

The name of a city ____________

The name of a country ____________

The name of a friend ____________

The last month of the year ____________

The day before Monday ____________

The name of a famous person ____________

The name of your school ____________

2 All your answers are **proper nouns**. Did you remember the **capital letters**? On the back of this sheet write some more **proper nouns**.

Name ______________________________ Date ____________

Proper nouns

People's names, places, days of the week and months of the year are **proper nouns**. All **proper nouns** start with a **capital letter**.

1 The **proper nouns** in this story are in the wrong places. Underline all the **proper nouns**.

The school trip

My name is Buckingham Palace. My school is Mrs Wright. It is in a town called Monday. My teacher's name is London. On Sam, the first day of the school week, our teacher told us we were going to Hill Top School to see the Queen. She lives in Upford.

The next day we all set off in the coach. Our teacher pointed out lots of interesting things to see. We saw the River Big Ben, and a famous clock called Thames.

2 Write out the story, putting the correct **proper nouns** in the right places.

Name ______________________ Date ______________

Common nouns and proper nouns

A **common noun** is the name of something. **Proper nouns** start with a **capital letter** and are people's names, places, days of the week and months of the year.

1 Circle all the **nouns** in the sentences.

The dog saw the cat on the wall and began to chase it.

Mr Martin dropped his glasses and bumped into a tree.

On Saturday, the footballer kicked the ball into the goal.

The baby in the pram had two teddies and a rattle.

2 Make up five sentences using these **nouns**.

rocket moon monster

____

bike boy accident

____

ship storm January

____

tiger jungle river

____

3 On the back of this sheet, write some **nouns** with 3, 4, 5, 6 and 7 letters. What is the longest **noun** you know?

Name ______________________ Date ____________

Common nouns and proper nouns

A **common noun** is the name of something. **Proper nouns** start with a **capital letter** and are people's names, places, days of the week and months of the year.

1 Sort out the **proper nouns** from the **common nouns**.

footpath	norton castle	east street	church
museum	river dabble	westbridge	playground
cemetery	sports centre	ashley park	wickton

Proper nouns ________ ________ ________

________ ________ ________

Common nouns ________ ________ ________

________ ________ ________

2 Label the **proper nouns** on the town map.

Map of ____________________

Name ______________________ Date __________

Diagnostic assessment – Verbs

Underline the **verbs** in the sentences.

I ran to the shop.

He ate all the sweets.

The dog hid the bone.

The bird flew over the hedge.

The boy lost his book.

Set A pages 10 - 11

Underline the **verbs**.

sit cat run bad dog hop cut door eat

happy me look run clap what his play

Set B pages 12 - 13

Write a **verb** to go with each of these words.

_______ slowly _______ hungrily _______ sadly

_______ quickly _______ quietly _______ loudly

Set C pages 14 - 15

Name ______________________________ Date ____________

Verbs

Verbs are action words – *walk*, *catch* and *eat* are all **verbs**.

1 The **verbs** under the pictures are in the wrong places.
Write the correct **verb** under each picture.

sit

____

hop

____

climb

____

swim

____

dig

____

skip

____

run

____

jump

____

2 What can you do?

I can ______________________ I can ______________________

______________________ ______________________

______________________ ______________________

______________________ ______________________

Name ______________________ Date ____________

Verbs

Verbs are action words – *walk*, *catch* and *eat* are all **verbs**.

Choose the best **verbs** to go in the sentences.

jump hop fly sing run purr

sleep bark squeak climb dig

A  can ______ and ______ .

A  can ______ and ______ .

A  can ______ and ______ .

A  can ______ and ______ .

A  can ______ and ______ .

A  can ______ and ______ .

A  can ______ and ______ .

I can ______ and ______ and ______ and ______ .

Name ______________________________ Date ____________

Verbs

Verbs are action words – *sleep*, *yawn* and *snore* are all **verbs**.

1 To find the treasure, think of **verbs** to put in the spaces.

Sail to Treasure Island.

________ at Sandy Bay.

________ north to the large cave.

________ right and walk to the rocks.

________ to the top of the rocks.

________ towards the volcano.

________ a line from the volcano to the tree.

________ half way along the line.

________ with a cross.

________ for the treasure.

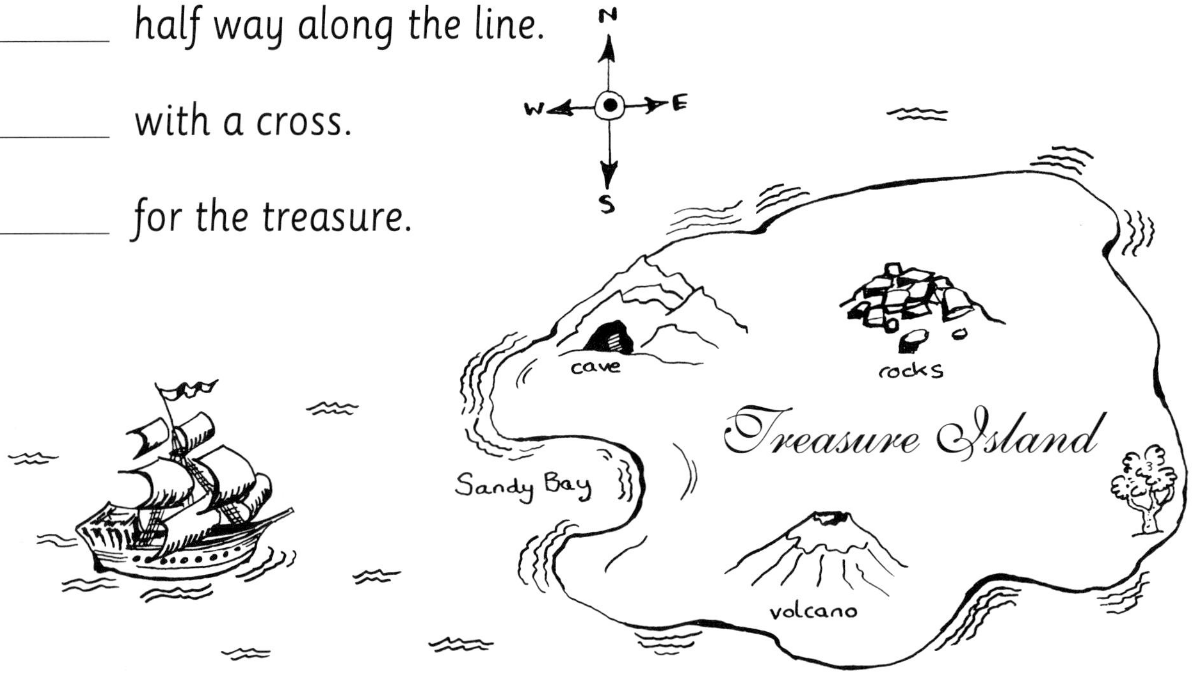

2 On the back of this sheet, write the instructions for getting back to the ship. Underline the **verbs** in your instructions.

Name ____________________ Date __________

Verbs

Verbs are action words – *sleep*, *yawn* and *snore* are all **verbs**.

In the sentences below, the printer has made some mistakes.
Write sensible **verbs** in place of the nonsense **verbs**.

1 The old lady poggled along the road.

2 The duck zimped into the pond.

3 The tree cragged over in the storm.

4 The car clud along the motorway.

5 The teacher mizzled the children a question.

6 The horse trunkled over the hedge.

7 The cat hoobed a little mouse.

8 The police officer strint the thief.

9 The boys brobbled when their team won.

10 The girls flonged at the funny clown.

Name ______________________________ Date ______________

Verbs

Verbs are action words – *draw*, *cook* and *grow* are all **verbs**.

1 The **verbs** in this story are muddled. Underline the **verbs**.

Mum cried the baby in the pram.

Then they sat to the park.

Mum stopped the pram up the hill.

She put on a bench and heard the paper.

The brakes of the pram pushed faulty.

The pram were down the hill towards the pond.

The baby ran loudly and Mum went the baby.

She rolled down the hill.

She read the pram just in time.

2 Write out the story, putting the **verbs** in the correct places.

Name ______________________________ Date ____________

Verbs

Verbs are action words – *draw*, *cook* and *grow* are all **verbs**.

1 Write the correct **verb** in the spaces.

asked shouted cried called replied pleaded

explained muttered whispered complained

"What did you do in school today?" __________ Mum.

"Please don't make me eat that spinach," __________ the boy.

"This bread is stale," __________ the old lady.

"Sssh, I'll tell you a secret," __________ Sam.

"My phone number is 543876," __________ the man.

"I've cut my knee," __________ the child.

"Get down from that tree," __________ Dad.

"I don't much like Aunt Aggie," __________ Mary.

"Can you hear me?" __________ Tom.

"The swimming pool is next to the school," __________ Jo.

2 On the back of this sheet, make up sentences using the following **verbs**.

answered yelled roared neighed

Name ______________________________ Date ______________

Diagnostic assessment – Adjectives

Underline the **adjectives** in the sentences.

The old man sat on the wooden bench.

The tiny puppy chewed the smelly sock.

The fierce lion ran after the little zebra.

The kind policeman helped the lost boy.

Set A
pages 17 - 18

Underline the **adjectives**.

table run happy cold book eat pretty green

school new skip high queen water read big

Set B
pages 19 - 20

Write an **adjective** to go with each noun.

________ rabbit	________ dinosaur	________ bike
________ shark	________ football	________ disco
________ cave	________ rainbow	________ desert

Set C
pages 21 - 22

Name ______________________ Date ____________

Adjectives

Adjectives tell us more about nouns – *sad* girl, *happy* boy.

1 The **adjectives** under the pictures are in the wrong places. Write the correct **adjective** under the picture.

sad ____________

happy ____________

cross ____________

cold ____________

hot ____________

dirty ____________

sleepy ____________

ugly ____________

2 Choose **adjectives** to describe these nouns.

____________ sun ____________ ice-cream

____________ trainers ____________ flower

____________ children ____________ horse

Name ______________________ Date ____________

Adjectives

Adjectives tell us more about nouns – *sad* girl, *happy* boy.

1 Look at these monsters. Choose **adjectives** to complete the sentences.

A This monster is __________. It has a __________ hat.

B This monster is __________. It has a __________ hat.

C This monster is __________. It has a __________ hat.

D This monster is __________. It has a __________ hat.

E This monster is __________. It has a __________ hat.

2 Draw a monster. Write some **adjectives** to describe it.

Name ____________________ Date ____________

Adjectives

Adjectives tell us more about nouns – *good* dog, *bad* cat.

1 Write **adjectives** that are opposite in meaning.

big

____

long

____

____

asleep

wet __________

full

____

up

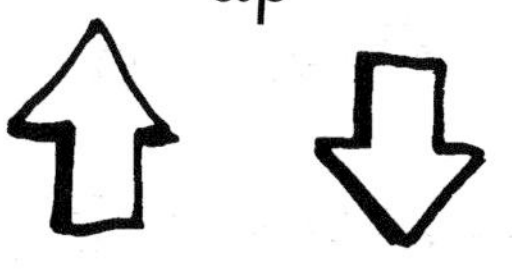

____

2 Join the opposite **adjectives**.

over	far
first	narrow
wide	under
heavy	quiet
loud	light
near	last

3 Use the **adjectives** above to complete these sentences.

The brick is ________ but the feather is ________ .

The road is ________ but the path is ________ .

The winner is ________ but the loser is ________ .

Name ______________________ Date ____________

Adjectives

Adjectives tell us more about nouns – *good* dog, *bad* cat.

1 Write **adjectives** to finish the sentences.

The elephant is big and __________ .

The lion is hungry and __________ .

The giraffe is graceful and __________ .

The rabbit is timid and __________ .

The dog is friendly and __________ .

2 Join the similar **adjectives**.

right →	cruel
unkind	haughty
brave	correct
small	last
swift	silly
final	tiny
foolish	fearless
proud	fast

3 Choose **adjectives** from above to go with these **nouns**.

__________ car __________ lion

__________ knight __________ eagle

__________ mouse __________ peacock

Name ______________________________ Date ____________

Adjectives

Adjectives tell us more about nouns – *beautiful* flower, *exciting* book.

1 Think of **adjectives** to describe these **nouns**.

ancient

castle

knight

forest

dragon

2 Read the story below and write **adjectives** in the spaces.

Once upon a time there was a ________ dragon. He lived in a ________ forest near a ________ castle. In the castle lived a ________ knight. One day the ________ dragon captured a ________ princess. The ________ knight heard the cries of the ________ princess and he set off to rescue her. He rode through the ________ forest until he came to a ________ cave.

He could see the ________ princess and the ________ dragon.

"Fear not, ________ princess," said the ________ knight. "I have come to rescue you."

"Don't bother," said the ________ princess, "life is much more fun living here in the ________ forest with the ________ dragon than living in your ________ castle."

Name ____________________ Date ____________

Adjectives

Adjectives tell us more about nouns – *beautiful* flower, *exciting* book.

1 Look at the people in the rogues gallery. Write an **adjective** for each noun.

Cut throat Jake	Evil Enid	Swag bag Pete
________ head	________ nose ring	________ moustache
________ glasses	________ teeth	________ ears
________ lips	________ hair	________ smile
________ scar	________ eyes	________ nose

2 Choose one of the rogues and put the description into the police report.

"I was proceeding down the High Street when I saw the suspect carrying a suspicious parcel. He turned and looked at me and I was able to note his features. He had:

____

____

____

____

____

It is my belief that the burglar is ____________________

Signed PC Catchem

Name ______________________________ Date ______________

Diagnostic assessment – Adverbs

Underline the **adverbs** in the sentences.

He cried sadly.

She ran quickly.

They walked slowly.

The man spoke crossly.

Set A pages 24 - 25

Circle the **adverbs**.

sadly here in quickly slowly house man

walk easily happily swing hat dance suddenly

strong strongly silently window sang sweetly

Set B pages 26 - 27

Write an **adverb** to go with each of these verbs.

walked __________ crept __________ listened __________

waited __________ smiled __________ cried __________

laughed __________ sang __________ whispered __________

Set C pages 28 - 29

Name ______________________________ Date ______________

Adverbs

Adverbs tell us more about verbs – run *quickly*, walk *slowly*.

1 Underline the **adverbs** in the sentences.

She swam quickly.

The dog barked loudly.

She read the book carefully.

He won the race easily.

The giant ate greedily.

2 Choose an **adverb** to complete each sentence below.

quickly	nicely	loudly	carefully
slowly	neatly	softly	quietly

I like to run ________________.

I like to talk ________________.

I like to sing ________________.

I like to draw ________________.

I like to work ________________.

Name ______________________________ Date ______________

Adverbs

Adverbs tell us more about verbs – run *quickly*, walk *slowly*.

1 Underline the correct **adverbs** in each sentence.

The  flew loudly / swiftly.

The  cried quietly / loudly.

The  moved swiftly / slowly.

The  talked brightly / quietly.

The  raced slowly / speedily.

The  shouted speedily / angrily.

The  shone angrily / brightly.

2 Underline the **adverbs**.

The lion roared fiercely.

The horse galloped quickly.

The door opened suddenly.

The rain fell softly.

The boy walked slowly.

Name ______________________________ Date ______________

Adverbs

Adverbs tell us more about verbs – sneezed *loudly*, whispered *quietly*.

Change the words in the brackets to **adverbs**.

Once upon a time there was a boy called Jack. He lived (happy) __________ with his mother. One day he found his mother crying (bitter) __________ .

"What is the matter?" asked Jack.

"We have no money and soon we will starve," replied Jack's mother (sad) ________ . "You must go and sell our cow in the market."

Jack set off (immediate) ____________ and soon he met an old woman.

"Will you sell me that cow for five magic beans?" she asked Jack.

"Yes," said Jack, and he took the beans and ran (swift) __________ home to his mother.

His mother was angry when she saw the beans and she threw them out of the window. In the night the beans began to grow (rapid) __________ and by morning they had grown up into the sky.

When Jack saw the beanstalk he decided to climb up it. He went (careful) __________ up to the top. At the top was a castle that belonged to a giant.

Jack crept (quiet) __________ up to the door of the castle. He could see a giant sleeping (sound) __________ and the giant's wife baking some bread. Jack was (ravenous) ______________ hungry. He looked (hungry) __________ at the bread.

(Sudden) ______________ the giant woke up and saw Jack at the door.

Name ______________________ Date ____________

Adverbs

Adverbs tell us more about verbs – sneezed *loudly*, whispered *quietly*.

1 Draw a line to the best **adverb** to finish the sentence.

The bird sang	patiently
The boy worked	quietly
The baby cried	loudly
The thief crept	sweetly
The man shouted	sneakily
The teacher whispered	heavily
The class waited	angrily
The tree fell	carefully

2 Choose three of the **adverbs** from the list above and write a sentence for each.

____

____

____

3 Answer the questions.

How did he speak? ______________

How did she run? ______________

How did he eat? ______________

How did she smile? ______________

How did they work? ______________

Name ______________________ Date ____________

Adverbs

Adverbs tell us more about verbs – cried *miserably*, laughed *happily*.

1 Write four **adverbs** for each of the verbs.

play

talk

write

eat

2 Choose the best **adverbs** to fill the gaps below.

angrily	loudly	frantically	sweetly	silently
gracefully	patiently	swiftly	fluently	immediately

He waited ____________ She sang ____________

He sneezed ____________ She ran ____________

He crept ____________ She danced ____________

He decided ____________ She wrote ____________

He waved ____________ She shouted ____________

3 Think of as many different **adverbs** as you can to describe the following verbs.

walked ______________________________

spoke ______________________________

read ______________________________

Name ______________________________ Date ____________

Adverbs

Adverbs tell us more about verbs – cried *miserably*, laughed *happily*.

Write an **adverb** of your choice in each of the spaces in this story.

The two boys were playing ________ in the garden. Suddenly the ground shook and a spaceship landed ________ beside them. Two green aliens stepped ________ out of the spaceship. One spoke ________ to the boys.

"Could you tell us how to get to your school?" he asked ________ .

"Why do you want to go there?" the boys answered ________ .

"Your teacher is our long-lost sister," said the aliens ________ .

The boys ________ told the aliens how to get to the school. When the spaceship had gone, one boy turned ________ to the other and said, "Well, I ________ thought Miss Marshun looked a bit peculiar."

"Yes," said the other boy ________ . She used to say she had eyes in the back of her head."

Then, both boys laughed ________ .

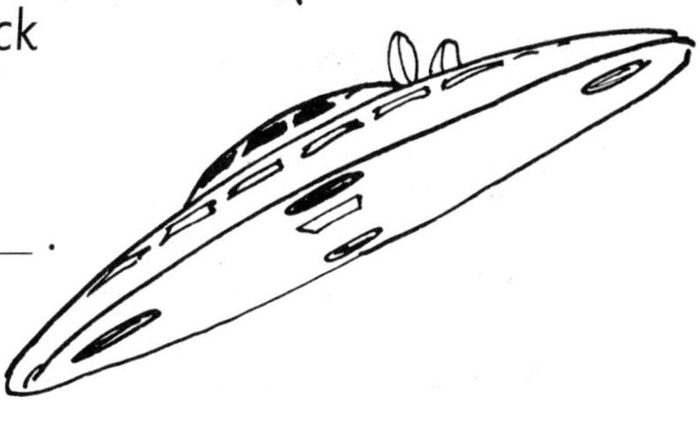

Name ______________________________ Date ____________

Diagnostic assessment – Pronouns

Match the nouns to the **pronouns**.

the man	it
the frog	he
the teachers	she
the woman	they

Set A
pages 31 - 32

Underline the **pronouns**.

The man went to the shop and he bought a paper.

They were happy when the team won.

The children saw the horse and wanted to stroke it.

Sophie can help him to mend the car.

The police gave them a reward.

Set B
pages 33 - 34

Write a **pronoun** in each sentence.

"Give _____ the ball," said the boy.

The girl lost _____ coat.

The children wanted _____ pocket money.

"Have you done _____ homework?" asked the teacher.

"That is _____ book but _____ can borrow _____."

Set C
pages 35 - 36

Name ______________________________ Date ____________

Pronouns

A **pronoun** is a word that is used instead of a noun.
The man ran – *He* ran. The girl clapped – *She* clapped.

1 Match the nouns to the **pronouns**.

the boy	she
the children	he
the girl	it
the mouse	they

2 In each sentence, write a **pronoun** instead of the noun.

Paul went to the match. ________ went to the match.

Ann went on the train. ________ went on the train.

The ball was in the goal. ________ was in the goal.

The friends went to the seaside. ________ went to the seaside.

3 Write a **pronoun** in each of the gaps.

The horse ran and ________ won the race.

Mary ate the big bun and then ________ felt sick.

Tom climbed up the tree but ________ could not get down.

The children went to school and ________ met a new teacher.

Name ______________________ Date ____________

Pronouns

A **pronoun** is a word that is used instead of a noun.
The man ran – *He* ran. The girl clapped – *She* clapped.

1 Underline the **pronouns**.

The girl saw the dog and she ran away.

The boy kicked the ball and he scored a goal.

The dog barked when it saw the man.

The children laughed when they saw the clown.

2 Write **pronouns** instead of the underlined nouns.

The prince saw the princess and the prince smiled.

____

The wolf chased the little goats and the wolf ate them.

____

The woman made a cake and then the woman ate the cake.

____

The boys made a car and the boys played in the car.

____

3 Circle the **pronouns**.

play he like she man it they happy

Name ______________________ Date ____________

Pronouns

> A **pronoun** is a word that is used instead of a noun.
> Give the book to John – Give *it* to *him*.

I you him her me us them

1 Write out the sentences, putting in the **pronouns**.

Mum said, "Mum will help."

Mum said, "I will help."

Dad saw Joe and gave Joe a present.

____

Jill said, "Help Jill to carry the bucket."

____

Jack and Jill said that the bucket was too heavy for Jack and Jill.

____

The children said, "The bus will take the children to school."

____

Mum put on Mum's coat.

____

2 Write a **pronoun** in each sentence.

"Give ______ the money," said the robber.

"Show ______ the way home," said the children.

"The little children are lost. Can ______ help them?"

"The man said, "Can ______ have an ice-cream?"

Mum gave ______ a new tie.

The girl gave ______ friend a biscuit.

Name ________________________ Date ____________

Pronouns

A **pronoun** is a word that is used **instead of a noun**.
Give the book to John – Give *it* to *him*.

1 Circle the **pronouns**.

She caught a fish.

He sang a song.

We went to the shops.

The teacher gave him homework.

They had a party.

Sam put her book on the table.

We will see the film tomorrow.

Mr Brown gave us some books.

"Will you stop talking," said Dad.

"That's my apple," said Tom.

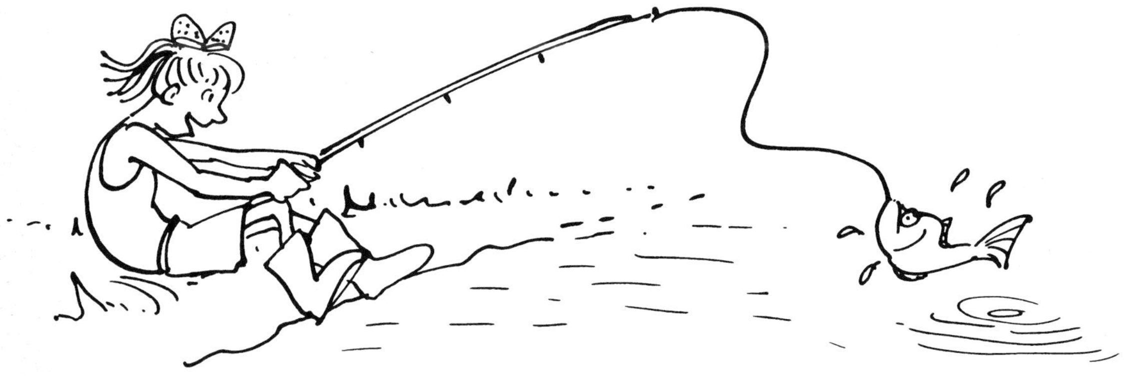

2 Underline the **silly pronouns**. Write a **sensible pronoun** in each sentence.

The girl ate its dinner. ________________

The man saw they friend. ________________

"That's him bike," said Tim. ________________

The teacher gave we a book. ________________

"Are I best friends?" ________________

Name ______________________ Date __________

Pronouns

> A **pronoun** is a word that is used **instead of a noun**.
> The children smiled at the baby – *They* smiled at *her*.

I they she he we it me him her us them

1 Write a **pronoun** in each gap.

________ have been to London.

________ is an old man.

________ must stop that.

________ are eating.

________ is a little girl.

________ are all in the room.

________ is nearly morning.

"Give it to ________ !" I said.

"Do you like ________?"

The police gave ________ directions.

"Have you seen ________?"

The children helped ________ to tidy up.

2 Join the related **pronouns**.

I	his	mine	ourselves
he	me	hers	themselves
we	them	ours	himself
she	us	their	myself
they	her	him	herself

Name ______________________________ Date ______________

Pronouns

A **pronoun** is a word that is used **instead of a noun**.
The children smiled at the baby – *They* smiled at *her*.

1 Circle the **pronouns**.

he they cat near we and what us house him cut

you here it no but me I good do her his them

2 Write in the missing **pronouns**.

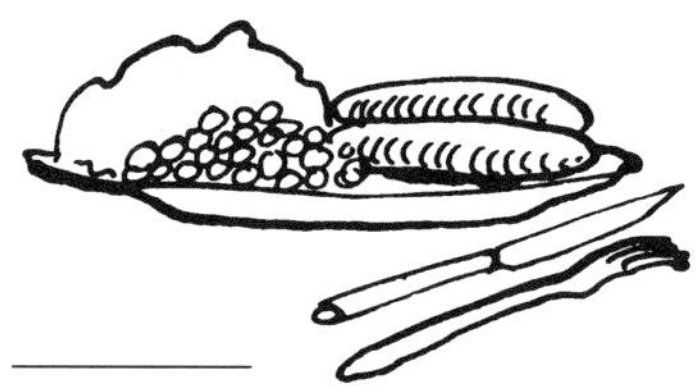

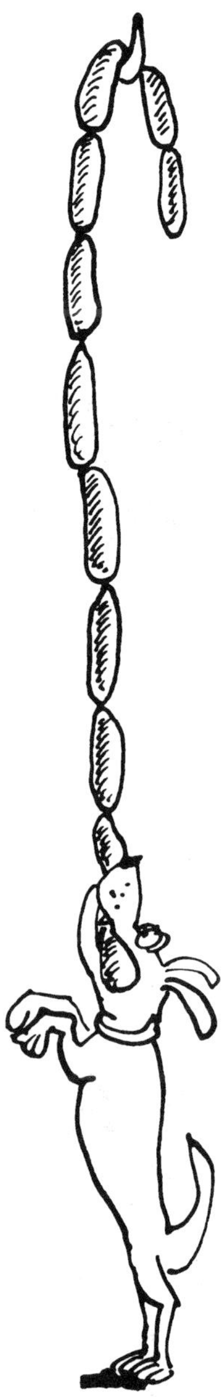

One day a man met an old lady in the woods. ______ gave ______ three wishes. The man hurried home to ______ wife. When he got home ______ was very hungry.

"Where is my supper?" ______ asked, but there was only a crust of bread for ______ supper.

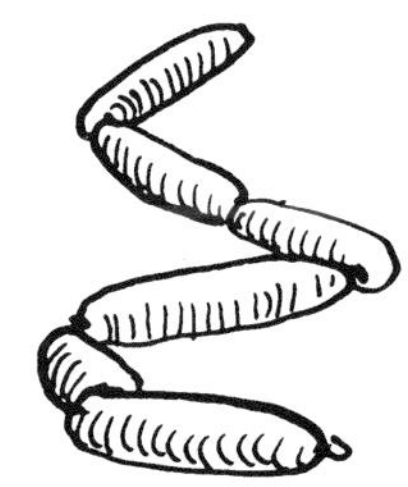

"______ wish ______ had a fat, juicy sausage," said the man and immediately a sausage appeared on ______ plate.

"Where did that sausage come from?" asked ______ wife.

So the man told ______ about the three wishes.

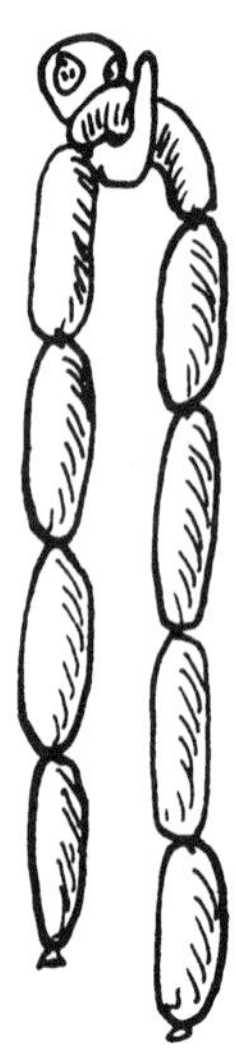

"You big fool," said ______ wife. "______ have wasted a wish. ______ wish that sausage was at the end of your nose."

At once the sausage appeared on the end of the man's nose. The man could not pull the sausage off ______ nose.

"______ wish ______ would go," ______ said desperately and the sausage disappeared.

"Now ______ have no wishes left," said his wife sadly.

Name ______________________ Date ____________

Diagnostic assessment – Prepositions

Underline the **prepositions.**

The hat is on the table.

The mouse is by the cheese.

The dragon is in the cave.

The cat is under the tree.

The dog ran up the path.

Set A pages 38 - 39

Write a **preposition** in each sentence.

She put her hands ____________ her head.

The train went ____________ the tunnel.

The children ran ____________ the hall.

The crab went ____________ the rock.

The dog barked ____________ the cat.

Set B pages 40 - 41

Choose three sensible **prepositions** for each sentence.

The baby sat ______ the mat. The girl is ______ the sea.
______ ______
______ ______

The cat jumped ______ the tree. The boy ran ______ the sand.
______ ______
______ ______

Set C pages 42 - 43

Name ________________________ Date ____________

Prepositions

Prepositions show the **link** between two or more things.
The cat sat *on* the mat. The cat is *by* the mat.

1 Look at the picture. Write a **preposition** in each space.

The boy is ______ the swing.

The sand pit is ______ the slide.

The girl is ______ the slide.

The boy is ______ the slide.

The baby is ______ the pram.

The mother is ______ the tree.

2 Write these **prepositions** on the picture.

up on by in under down

Name ______________________________ Date ____________

Prepositions

Prepositions show the **link** between two or more things.
The cat sat *on* the mat. The cat is *by* the mat.

1 Underline the **prepositions**.

The cow is in the field.
The book is on the table.
The boy is up the tree.
The girl is by the chair.
The bus went under the bridge.

2 Write a **preposition** in each gap.

The boy ran _____ the path.
The car was _____ the garage.
The picture is _____ the wall.
The house is _____ the sea.
The box is _____ the bed.

3 Write **prepositions** in these sentences.

along by up on under

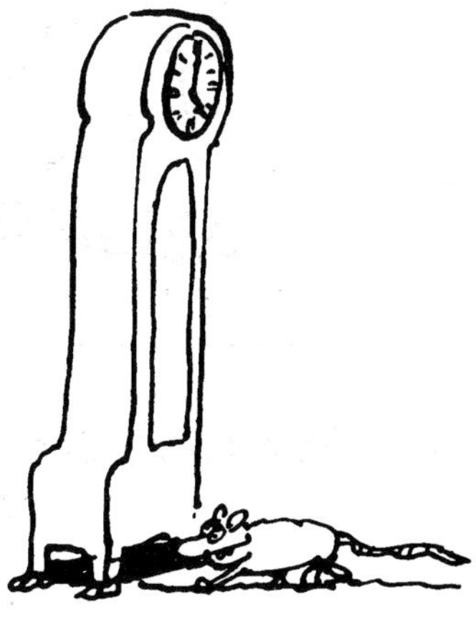

The mouse ran _______ the wall, ____ the chair leg and sat ______ the table. The cat saw the mouse _____ the cheese. The mouse ran away to its home ________ the clock.

Name ______________________________ Date ______________

Prepositions

Prepositions show the **link** between two or more things.
The river ran *under* the bridge. The bridge went *over* the river.

1 Underline the **prepositions**.

My mum is at work.

The child ran into the room.

He got ice-cream from the freezer.

The plane flew above the clouds.

The box sank below the waves.

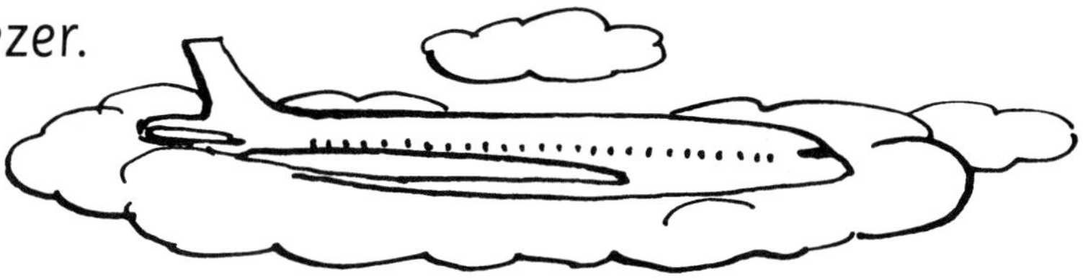

2 Choose the correct **preposition** for each sentence.

The letter is (below/from) America.

The ______________________________

The diver swam (at/under) the ship.

The ______________________________

The car ran (into/below) the lamp post.

The ______________________________

The kite flew (above/from) the tree.

The ______________________________

3 Write some **prepositions** in these sentences.

A boy went ______ the park. He saw a fish ______ the lake and he heard a bird singing ______ a tree ______ him. He took his camera ______ his bag and pointed it ____ the bird.

"This will make a good picture," he said.

Name ______________________ Date ____________

Prepositions

Prepositions show the **link** between two or more things.
The river ran *under* the bridge. The bridge went *over* the river.

1 Write these **prepositions** in the sentences.

with across around through near over off towards

The dog ran ________ the road.

The horse jumped ________ the fence.

The people got ________ the bus.

The child ran ________ her mum.

The path went ________ the wood.

The jogger ran ________ the lake.

The house is ________ the shops.

He liked to eat chips ________ fish.

2 Choose three suitable **prepositions** for each sentence.

The pencil was ________ the table.
____
____

The video was ________ the TV.
____
____

The ball went ________ the window.
____
____

The man walked ________ the lake.
____
____

Name ______________________________ Date ______________

Prepositions

Prepositions show us the link between two or more things.
She went *through* the gate. He ran *after* the horse.

1 Underline the **prepositions** in the silly sentences.

The child went through the slide.
He walked above the path.
She gave the present from her brother.
The car drove with the garage.
She hid over the tree.
The man went along the door.
He took the money when the bank.

2 Write the sentences, putting in sensible **prepositions**.

____
____
____
____
____
____
____

3 Complete the story using **prepositions**.

The dog chased the cat __________ the path, __________ the gate, __________ the garden, __________ the flower bed, __________ the lawn, __________ the trees, __________ the pond, __________ the house and __________ the cat flap.

Name ______________________ Date ____________

Prepositions

Prepositions show us the link between two or more things.
She went *through* the gate. He ran *after* the horse.

1 Underline the ten **prepositions**.

the inside who you into under when we
house between near so we on in
how through here above over

2 Choose a **preposition** and then complete each sentence.

The boy watched the river flowing under the bridge.

The horse ran ______________________

The path went ______________________

The plane flew ______________________

The rabbit jumped ______________________

The giant slept ______________________

You will find the treasure ______________________

She put her painting ______________________

It was quite dry ______________________

The house was ______________________

3 Choose two **prepositions** and write a sentence for each.

____

____

Name ______________________________ Date ______________

Diagnostic assessment – Conjunctions

Underline the **conjunctions**.

The pot and the pan were on the cooker.

The teacher gave Sam and Peter the books.

You can go out but don't play near the pond.

I like football but I don't like tennis.

Set A

pages 45 - 46

Fill in the gaps.

before after if when where because

I like running ________ I am good at it.

I eat scones ______ I am at my gran's.

______ you have your arm bands you can go swimming.

Put the paper in the bin ______ you have opened the ice-cream.

Meet me in the playground ______ school begins.

That is the field ______ the horse lives.

Set B

pages 47 - 48

Circle the **conjunctions**.

until red although book sailing unless

after because quickly while if eating before

where clock read when

Set C

pages 49 - 50

Name ______________________ Date ______________

Conjunctions

Conjunctions join words and sentences.
Cup *and* saucer. He was tall *but* he was not fat.

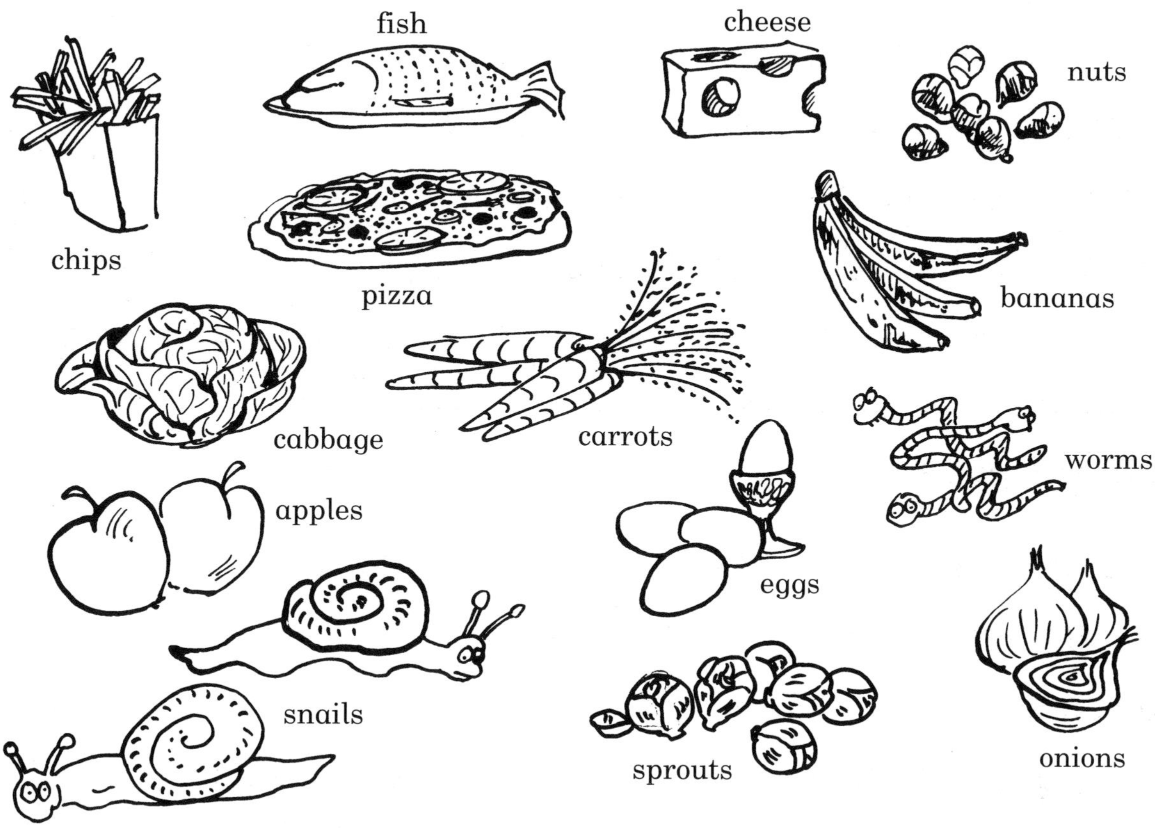

Complete the sentences, then underline the **conjunctions**.

I like eating __________ and I like eating __________.

I like eating __________ and I like eating __________.

I like eating __________ and I like eating __________.

I like eating __________ but I don't like eating __________.

I like eating __________ but I don't like eating __________.

I like eating __________ but I don't like eating __________.

Name ______________________________ Date ____________

Conjunctions

Conjunctions join words and sentences.
Cup *and* saucer. He was tall *but* he was not fat.

1 Join the opposites.

high →	low
in	over
under	out
come	down
inside	go
up	outside

2 Join the pairs using *and*.

high and ______ up ______ ______

in ______ ______ under ______ ______

come ______ ______ inside ______ ______

3 Fill in the gaps and join the sentences using *but*.

I can go up but I can't go ______.

I can go high ______ I can't go ______.

I can go ______ ______ I can't go outside.

I can go under ______ I can't go ______.

I can go ______ ______ I can't go out.

Name ______________________________ Date ____________

Conjunctions

Conjunctions join words and sentences.
In *and* out. You can play *after* lunch.

1 Write *and* or *but* in each sentence.

I like to eat fish _____ chips.

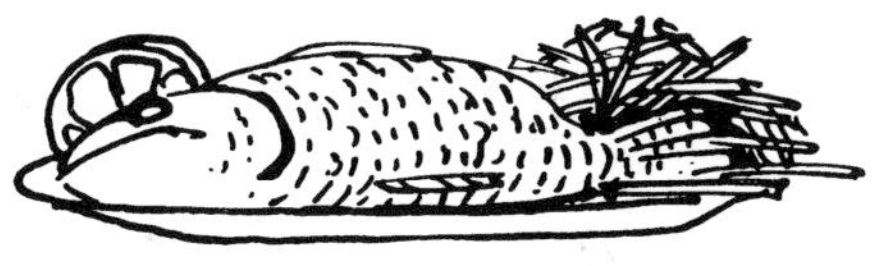

I like to eat carrots _____ I don't like beans.

Mum bought crisps _____ a fizzy drink.

Can you see all the cars _____ buses?

Dad can swim _____ I can't.

Don't forget your coat, boots _____ hat.

This room is big _____ that room is small.

Can you pat your head _____ rub your tum?

Bring your pencil _____ leave your bag.

Jack is tall _____ Joe is small.

2 Write *before* or *after* in each sentence.

Put on your coat _______ you go out.

Close the drawer _______ you have taken out the pencil.

Take off your socks _______ you wash them.

Unpack the shopping _______ you have been to the shops.

Name ______________________ Date ______________

Conjunctions

Conjunctions join words and sentences.
In *and* out. You can play *after* lunch.

1 Use these **conjunctions** to fill the gaps in the sentences.

when because if where

I can do it ________ you will help me.

This is the box ________ we keep the pencils.

This coat must be yours ________ it has your name on it.

I will have my lunch ________ I have done all my work.

He went by plane ________ it was quicker.

________ you take that road you will avoid the traffic.

To see an iceberg, you must travel to ________ it is cold.

The girls were going home ________ we saw them.

2 Circle the **conjunctions**.

and mat swim but when before stand if it

over after cup because tree where walked

Name ______________________________ Date ______________

Conjunctions

> **Conjunctions** join words and sentences. Go to the shop *before* you come home. Don't be late *because* Jane is coming.

1 Write out each sentence with the correct **conjunction**.

Eat the crisps before/after you open the packet.

____

Eat the oranges but/because leave the apple.

____

Brush your teeth before/and going to bed.

____

You can watch TV because/if you have been good.

____

Keep running until/when you pass the finishing line.

____

You can have an ice-cream if/after you like.

____

The man showed us where/while he lived.

____

2 Choose different **conjunctions** and finish the sentences.

She smiled ______________________________

She smiled ______________________________

He shouted ______________________________

He shouted ______________________________

Name ________________________________ Date ______________

Conjunctions

Conjunctions join words and sentences. Go to the shop *before* you come home. Don't be late *because* Jane is coming.

1 Fill in the gaps with the correct **conjunctions**.

because unless and although until while

He chose a different way __________ the motorway was busy.

You cannot go to the cinema ________ you can afford it.

Wait in the playground ________ the coach arrives.

He liked to do judo ______ karate.

My Gran can knit ________ she watches TV.

She climbed the rocks _________ she had been told to wait.

2 Make three sentences using different **conjunctions**.

The audience left the theatre _________ the play had ended.

____

____

Dragons like princesses _________ they are tasty.

____

____

The cat goes out __________ it is dark.

____

____

Name ______________________________ Date ______________

Diagnostic assessment – Subject and verb agreement

Circle the right **verb**.

I am/are sad. She are/is happy. It is/am dirty.

He is/are fit. You are/is well. They are/is nice.

Set A
pages 52 - 53

Circle the right **verb**.

I was/were going to school.

He were/was playing football.

We was/were swimming.

You were/was on the bus.

They were/was watching television.

Set B
pages 54 - 55

Circle the right **verb**.

Jo and Pip were/was at the zoo.

The keeper was/were feeding the lions.

"Is/are it dangerous in there?" asked Jo.

"If you were/was to come in it would be dangerous," said the keeper, "but I am OK."

Just then a big lion ate the keeper.

"Is/are you still OK?" asked Pip.

Set C
pages 56 - 57

Name ______________________ Date ____________

Subject and verb agreement

Example: She *is* good. ✓ She *are* good. ✗

1 Choose the correct sentence and write it on the line.

He is happy. He are happy.

They is sad. They are sad.

We is lost. We are lost.

It is late. It are late.

You is well. You are well.

She are tall. She is tall.

2 Circle the right word.

I am / are clever. We are / am hungry.

You are / is hot. They is / are good.

He is / am cross. She is / are sleepy.

It is / am dark. It are / is cold.

Name ______________________________ Date ______________

Subject and verb agreement

Example: She *is* good. ✓ She *are* good. ✗

1 Join the words to make some sentences.

I	is	happy.
He	are	sad.
She	am	lost.
It	are	good.
We	is	tall.
You	are	late.
They	is	clever.

2 Now write the sentences.

I ______________________________

He ______________________________

She ______________________________

It ______________________________

We ______________________________

You ______________________________

They ______________________________

Don't forget the full stops.

Name ______________________________ Date ____________

Subject and verb agreement

Example: I *have* a pen. ✓ I *has* a pen. ✗

1 Choose the correct **verb**.

If you go/goes down there you will get to the river.

____

I hope/hopes that you like cycling.

____

We runs/run every evening.

____

My friend and I like/likes to read in the book corner.

____

You is/are going to see the doctor tomorrow.

____

The girl write/writes well.

____

The boy has/have won a medal.

____

2 Underline the mistakes in the sentences.

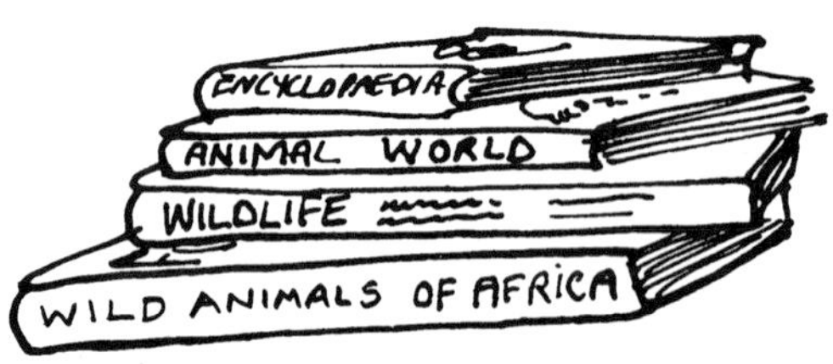

Library Time

I likes it when it are library time because we can choose three books. I choose books about animals because I loves animals. When I gets my books I takes them to show my teacher. Then I sits and reads them.

Name ______________________ Date __________

Subject and verb agreement

Example: I *was* sleepy. ✓ I *were* sleepy. ✗

1 Make some sentences.

I	were	sleeping	quickly.
You	was	eating	quietly.
He	were	running	soundly.
It	were	singing	noisily.
We	was	playing	dangerously.
They	was	talking	sweetly.

2 Write the sentences you have made.

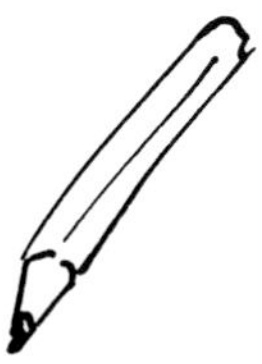

____

____

____

____

____

____

Don't forget the full stops.

Name ______________________ Date ____________

Subject and verb agreement

Example: *I* was going. ✓ You *was* going. ✗

1 The computer at the police station has got a virus. When a police officer typed in an interview, some of the subjects and verbs didn't agree. Underline the mistakes in the dialogue.

"Where was you last night?"
"I were at home."
"Was you at home all night?"
"No. I goes out to see my friend."
"What time were that?"
"It were nearly ten o'clock."
"Funny that – it were half past ten when the old lady lost her purse!"
"I never takes her purse!"
"I know you didn't. You must be the young man who help her to pick up all her money."
"How does you know about that?"
"The old lady tells us about a nice kind man who was helping her. Well done lad!"

2 Write the young man's answers with the correct **verbs**.

Name ______________________ Date ____________

Subject and verb agreement

Example: I *go* to the shops. ✓ I *goes* to the shop. ✗

1 Write a suitable **pronoun** in the first space and finish the sentences.

________ is ______________________

________ are ______________________

________ am ______________________

________ like ______________________

________ likes ______________________

________ have ______________________

________ has ______________________

________ go ______________________

________ goes ______________________

2 Fill in the gaps with *was* or *were*.

Jack and Dan ______ hungry but Dan ______ hungrier than Jack. They ______ looking for something to eat. Dan ______ looking in the cupboard while Jack ______ searching in the fridge. Then Jack saw something. It ______ a big jelly. They ______ both delighted and shared the jelly between them.

Name ______________________________ Date ______________

Diagnostic assessment – Sentence practice

Answer the questions.

The dog ran after the long stick.

Which word is the verb? __________

Which two words are nouns? __________ __________

Which word is an adjective? __________

Set A
pages 59 - 60

Answer the questions.

The proud prince put the gold crown on his head and went slowly down the steps.

Which four words are nouns? ______ ______ ______ ______

Which two words are adjectives? ______ ______

Which word is a pronoun? ______

Which word is an adverb? ______

Set B
pages 61 - 62

Write three sentences. These words might help you.

boy clever quickly ran into in under dog lively
quietly jumped under girl sleepy swam water tree
sadly baby school naughty bridge crawled slowly

	adjective	noun	verb	preposition		noun
The					the	
The					the	
The					the	

Set C
pages 63 - 64

Name ______________________ Date ______________

Sentence practice

1 Find ten **nouns** in the picture.

___________ ___________ ___________ ___________ ___________

___________ ___________ ___________ ___________ ___________

2 Make up five sentences with **nouns** and **verbs** to describe the picture.

fishing eating swimming flying rowing

1 ____

2 ____

3 ____

4 ____

5 ____

Name ______________________ Date ____________

Sentence practice

1 Sort out the muddled **adjectives**.

a happy tree ______________________

a tall baby ______________________

the hot freezer ______________________

the cold sun ______________________

a dry toy ______________________

a soft desert ______________________

a rainy door ______________________

a glass day ______________________

2 Add a suitable **adverb**.

quickly slowly kindly badly sweetly loudly

The snail moved ________ along the path.

The dog fell and hurt its leg ________.

The bird sang ________ in the tree.

The old lady ________ gave them an ice-cream.

The lion roared ________ from its rock.

The rabbit ran ________ into its hole.

Name ______________________________ Date ______________

Sentence practice

1 Make the sentences using these parts of speech.

	noun	verb	preposition		noun
The	giant	lives	in	the	castle.
The				the	.
The				a	.
The				the	.
The				a	.

2 Now add an **adjective** to your **noun** and an **adverb** to your **verb**.

	adjective	noun	verb	adverb	preposition		noun
The	hungry	giant	lives	happily	in	the	castle
The						the	.
The						a	.
The						the	.
The						a	.

Name ______________________________ Date ____________

Sentence practice

1 The computer has failed to write some words in these sentences. Write in the missing letters.

The tree fell d________ in the st________ wind.

The elephant walked sl_______ through the d_______ jungle.

The cat jumped _____ the tree.

The lion stealthily wa________ towards its prey.

The plane flew ab______ the clouds.

The snake slid ac________ the ground.

The spider qui________ caught the t_____ y fly.

The frog hopped eas________ over the beaut_________ lily pads.

The sun shone bri__________ in the clear bl_____ sky.

The farmer care__________ dug up the val__________ treasure _____ his meadow.

2 Can you find the following in the sentences above?

8 nouns	6 adjectives	8 verbs	5 adverbs	5 prepositions

Name ______________________ Date ____________

Sentence practice

1 Match the beginnings and endings of the sentences and put in suitable missing words.

The _____ (adjective) baby laughed	although he knew _____ (pronoun) should be quiet.
The bird flew _____ (adverb) over the hill	_____ (conjunction) he was being tickled.
The _____ (adjective) boy shouted	and landed gently on the _____ (noun).
You can _____ (verb) outside	before you go to _____ (noun).
You should clean your _____ (noun)	if it has stopped raining.

2 Write out your sentences.

____

____

____

____

____

Name ____________________ Date ____________

Sentence Practice

1 Sort out the correct word order.

sore licked paw his

The sad lion ____________________

fox crafty quickly away the from

The rabbit ran ____________________

frog but leapt the river into the

The snake slid towards the frog ____________________

river through trees the until reached it the

The huge dinosaur crashed ____________________

his book reading bed went to and new

The boy finished ____________________

caught thief the and by him shop the

The policeman chased ____________________

2 Fill in the chart below using the sentences above.

6 nouns	5 verbs	4 conjunctions	3 prepositions	5 adjectives